# The Delphi Series
# Volume I

featuring

Anna Leahy,
Karen L. George, &
Robert Perry Ivey

Published by Blue Lyra Press

Copyright © 2016, 2019 BLUE LYRA PRESS
All rights reserved.

ISSN: 2167-8243, 2nd Edition
ISBN: 978-0692598900

*Blue Lyra Review*, a division of *Blue Lyra Press*, is currently closed to new submissions.

*Blue Lyra Press* publishes every spring/summer and accepts poetry and flash fiction chapbook submissions under 25 pages during two months throughout each year: January and July only. Send directly to the email below.

Writings or images published on the *Blue Lyra Review* website or in print are copyrighted by the creators. Explicit permission must be obtained from the copyright holder for use of any such material. E-mail bluelyrareview@gmail.com to obtain contact information for those writers and artists.

*Blue Lyra Review* & *Blue Lyra Press* are independent and rely solely on the generosity of donations so **please support the arts: (www.bluelyrareview.com/donations/)**.

SUBMISSIONS: direct to email with bio, acknowledgments, and table of contents

FACEBOOK: www.facebook.com/BlueLyraReview

TWITTER: twitter.com/BlueLyraReview

PURCHASE: bluelyrapress.com/

CORRESPONDENCE: **bluelyrareview@gmail.com**

Front Cover Art: Robin Grotke, *Harbor Chair, Ocracoke, North Carolina*

Front Cover Design: Claire Zoghb

# NOTE TO READERS

It is my delight to introduce you to the first book in the Delphi Series. In fact, this is the 2nd printing with a new cover showcasing the amazing photographic talents of Robin Grotke! I hope you enjoy it as much as I do! This book consists of three separate chapbooks by three separate poets bound in one single volume. Why would anyone do this? Good question! I think you, the reader, picked this book up because you are interested in one of the poets within these bound pages. In doing so, you are now exposed to two other poets. Maybe you heard of them before you picked this book up; maybe you didn't. It's like getting 3 books for the price of 1!

Anna Leahy begins the three chapbooks with poems about the 19th-century model, Elizabeth Siddal, who also painted. In "A Version (*The Lady of Shalott*, 1953)," Leahy masterfully crafts images to bring us to re-see Siddal: "Death by heartbreak: / on a stool at her loom / in a tower on an island, / out the window through the mirror, / turns her head, sees him ride / away, further and farther. / The great unraveling: / from her hands all the threads, / in the mirror all the cracking, / on the floor, on the shelf, / the crucifix repeats itself." She draws us through these persona poems, captivating the reader. "On Not Being *St. Cecilia* (1857)", Leahy lyrically writes, "Like birds, her fingertips light on the keys. / She's tuned and plays out of mind, out of sight / like crickets near dusk or owls dark at night."

Karen L. George brings the reader along a trail of heartfelt memories filled with loss and beauty. The opening poem eloquently foreshadows with "Hiking high on a ridge, a clearing in the storied forest. Flat river rocks on the ground in an arc— Moon come to Earth. You inch off the path." In my favorite, "Past Life Flash at Feast of the Flowering Moon, Chillicothe, Ohio," George gives us this movie-reel snippet that is a wonderful dancing blur: "I inhale sage smoke, feel grass blades tickle, the cool May ground rumble... my vision curls closed like the end chamber of a kaleidoscope rotates, spirals to a point of no light, a silent scene appears as on a movie screen, swatches of blurred motion focuses to a girl." George's poems show us scenes of hiking, traffic light waiting, trees on the way to work, ICU, and empty bedrooms, but always come back to focus on "the girl" and the raw emotions. These prose poems simmer then boil.

Robert Perry Ivey bookends the series with lovely, sorrowful poems about his daughter. These are brave poems, open love letters, and elegies that are in their essence about love and hope. In the opening poem, Ivey immediately lets the reader know this when he writes, "that switch they tell you about, / the one you can never understand, flips on love / like velvet on a dry tongue, strong like / love for the first time, but now, every day, / something closer than the words we have for all that is good, / something pure." Truly, these poems are pure beauty.

So, lean in, curl up to the pages, and sit down to these three poets on a welcoming chair at the end of a quiet pier.

# Table of Contents

Sharp Miracles by Anna Leahy      1

The Fire Circle by Karen L. George      27

Letters to my Daughter by Robert Perry Ivey      49

Critical Praise      77

# Sharp Miracles

by

# Anna Leahy

# Table of Contents

| | |
|---|---|
| Acknowledgments | 5 |
| A Note on the Text | 6 |
| Incantation | 8 |
| [Untitled] | 9 |
| Remembering *Ophelia* (1852) | 10 |
| On Hair | 11 |
| To Sew | 12 |
| A Version (*The Lady of Shalott*, 1853) | 13 |
| On Being Renamed | 14 |
| On Sketching *Pippa Passing the Loose Women* (1855) | 15 |
| Laudanum | 16 |
| On Not Being *St. Cecilia* (1857) | 17 |
| On Being *St. Catherine* (1857) | 18 |
| When We Met Ourselves (*How They Met Themselves*, 1851-60) | 19 |
| On Motherhood | 20 |
| To Speak | 21 |
| The Coroner's Verdict (1862) | 22 |
| After Burial | 23 |

If I Had To Choose One Word    24

On Being *Beata Beatrix* (1870)    25

# Acknowledgments

*The Account: A Journal of Prose, Poetry, and Thought* "On Being Beata Beatrix (1870)"
*A Face To Meet the Faces* (University of Akron Press) "On Sketching *Pippa Passing the Loose Women* (1855)"
*Her Mark Calendar 2010* (Woman Made Gallery) "Incantation"
*Image: A Journal of Arts & Religion* "On Not Being St. Cecilia (1857)" appeared under the title "Saint Cecilia"
*Mayday* "Laudanum," "On Being St. Catherine (1857)," and "Remembering Ophelia (1852)"

Since *Sharp Miracles* was published, these poems, sometimes in different versions, have been included in Leahy's full-length collection *Aperture,* available from Shearman Books.

# A Note on the Text

The opening epigraph is from Elizabeth Siddal's "Love and Hate," which is included in *Victorian Poetry and Poetic Theory* (Broadview, 1999).

Lizzie Siddal (1829-1862) was an artist's model, a painter, and a poet. She is the model in John Everett Millais's *Ophelia* and D. G. Rossetti's *How They Met Themselves, St. Catherine,* and *Beata Beatrix,* among other paintings and drawings by these and other Victorian artists. John Ruskin purchased several of Siddal's own paintings in 1855 and subsequently paid her a stipend for artwork she produced over several years. In 1860, after a long courtship during which she suffered intermittent ill health, Siddal married Pre-Raphaelite painter and poet D. G. Rossetti. After a stillbirth and becoming pregnant again, she died of a laudanum overdose.

Lucinda Hawksley's biography *Lizzie Siddal* (Walker & Co., 2004) was helpful to me in grappling with the facts of this woman's life.

*Open not thy lips, thou foolish one,*
*　　Nor turn to me thy face:*
*The blasts of heaven shall strike me down*
*　　Ere I will give thee grace.*

　　　　—*"Love and Hate," Elizabeth Siddal*

# Incantation

The tongue illuminates consequences:
        my words go and others' come back.

One thought leads to another and to sentences
        we must utter, mawing the syllables

to get them swaggering back and forth
        between our sizeable lives,

enchanted by the spell we cast
        with our sinny-shiny syntax,

because just when we hear our own voices—
        sometimes sibilant, often labial, unvoiced,

occasionally, wonderfully guttural—
        we find that we are listening, too.

Indeed, we are as interested in each other
        as we are in ourselves.

# [Untitled]

Need is a sharp miracle.

## Remembering *Ophelia* (1852)

I made a pretty painting,
secured a reputation
as demure as *Ophelia*. The secret
is the floaty-floaty feeling
and the shiver-chill
when the fire went out
under the tub
leaving my teeth to clatter;
that's what created my pallor,
gave the brush a goal.
I held my quiet pose, always anxious
for verbal intercourse, though not yet
for the real thing.

## On Hair

My red hair catches the eye.
I see it catch, like a spark.
I see the artist think it worth preserving
with oil or ink.
I made my way in millinery

>	(block-stitch-crown-brim
>	trim-skimming-primly
>	felt-feather-flower
>	flying off the hand
>	jagged cuticle catching).

I thought I had to.
Suddenly, I was eager
to be sketched—
and to sketch, myself.
I didn't know, though, that being inert
makes demands

>	(heart-heat-heft
>	weave-wend-weft
>	thread become strand).

**To Sew**

A pin is a too-thin mirror
       my image miniaturized
       between fingers.

Push through the fold of fabric—
       Push through—
       the little me quivering.

## A Version (*The Lady of Shalott*, 1853)

Death by heartbreak:
on a stool at her loom

in a tower on an island,
out the window through the mirror,

turns her head, sees him ride
away, farther and farther.

The great unraveling:
from her hands all the threads,

in the mirror all the cracking,
on the floor, on the shelf,

the crucifix repeats itself.
My hand directs her stare;

she's a looker, eyes open.
*What a delightful scene!*

**On Being Renamed**

It wasn't *Lizzie* that bothered me,
but his slashing off
the last letter of my last name.
      (My name is
      pinking sheared
      as if to keep from fraying.)
And the worry
that I might not hold up
to its new gentility,
that I was not enough or too much
of a good thing, that he would follow
his gaze
elsewhere, just when
I'd grown accustomed
to his looking.

**On Sketching *Pippa Passing the Loose Women* (1855)**

I drew people well. I drew
people out of themselves.
These are unrelated talents,
but I was happy to embody both.

I portrayed good Pippa and the prostitutes
equally ably, virgin and harlot alike.
I captured their expressions:
mutual curiosity, earnest interest.

Even the geese stretched to see.
I rendered the human form well, too.
*Render:* to create a version,
to give something in return

like the women exchanging glances.
*Rend:* to slit, to split apart.

**Laudanum**

Tincture of opium: a suffusing
saturating permeating flood.

Over the counter,
from the grocer, the barber, the baker.
A painkiller, a cordial
for irritable babies and bedwetting toddlers,
to alleviate cough, gout, menopause,
rheumatism, ulcers, cramps, bruises.
Nothing anyone suffered
could not be cured by it.

Hard to know whether sadness
is cause or effect, whether jealousy
is warranted or wanted, whether fatigue
comes or goes as a result,
whether weight is a figment,
subject matter, weightless, a filament.

How much is enough?
A hundred in an evening will lead me
to the difference between
intransitive and transitive,

between *drop: slump, decline, fall, plunge*
and *drop: let go of, release.*

I am drawn, so drawn.
I still hear the pun.

## On Not Being *St. Cecilia* (1857)


Like birds, her fingertips light on the keys.
She's tuned and plays out of mind, out of sight
like crickets near dusk or owls dark at night.
She works up a sweat. She thinks she's a tree.
All limbs, Cecilia climbs into her tub:
the luminous steam rises like wings,
the water boils like flocks of geese. It stings
blisters like feathers, scabs like leaves. She scrubs.

When this wet widow rises from her bath,
she bends with the breeze, then returns to her bench.
Her fingers are finches singing a riff
so she can't hear what's coming, nor whose wrath.
And when the axe hits her neck, her woody stench
fills the unsung world with organ music.

**On Being *St. Catherine* (1857)**

I imagined myself on the way
to have my body stretched over the wheel,
not later,
when the angels came
with lightning that sent spikes and splinters
into the air. Blood everywhere.
I wouldn't have looked any happier then,
so it was a good thing
he painted the scene he painted:
my sulking self looking more pallid
than I knew, though if boredom
and the heft of such luxurious clothes
could kill, this painting
might have done me in.
When I am beheaded, I thought,
milk will flow from my veins.
It was a relief not to be myself,
to see someone else's

                future rising from me.

## When We Met Ourselves (*How They Met Themselves,* 1851-60)

I didn't need the inky doppelgangers
he made for us in Paris;
I wanted each of us to be enough for the other.
Is it me fainting upon seeing myself,

or myself causing me to stumble?
This canvas was his longing
for reincarnation—that we had been or would be
reborn as others—not the life we lived.

This was my honeymoon swoon:
reading aloud, sketching each other's likenesses,
painting together, eating supper, and relief
when we returned home to England,

to our everyday existence, each of us merely
a raised surface in that marital engraving.

**On Motherhood**


I wouldn't have known much
what to do,
            what to do,
though I pretended
for a short while
with the empty cradle by the rocking chair,
where I rock-rock-rocked.

            If only the moon weren't sheared,
            necessary as an icicle.
            If only the mind weren't pricked red,
            bled-threaded like a train of thought.

I left the lack of pinking up
for someone else to write—
and he knew
just what to do.

My desire became like that first posing:
what could I make of myself,
what could be stroked into being?

But I had long lost my ability
to sit, and my wanting—my wanting to want—
      came with disbelief
      I couldn't suspend.

**To Speak**

Language stops a bitter mist
        from prattle-stitching, my tongue
        gone frantic with the easy sky (a squall).

## The Coroner's Verdict (1862)

After much testimony during the inquest
and numerous individuals claiming

*no note, no self-injurious behavior,*
*no pessimism, no need to prevent proper burial,*

my undoing was rendered accidental,
as death was common with laudanum

and various snags I was thought to have—
after which I could be remembered

however one imagined.
Dream me up; imagine me now.

**After Burial**

Can you believe he exhumed me?
        Not me per se, but the poems

he'd buried with me when he thought
        sorrow could be as powerful as language,

only later to discover he was wrong,
        that sorrow was autumn in the heart,

and winter threatened to beget spring.

## If I Had To Choose One Word

*Cleave:* itself and its opposite, all at once.

## On Being *Beata Beatrix* (1870)


He captured more ecstasy than I had
mustered, frustrated by leaning forward
as if for a kiss, my lips parted, my eyes closed,
my mind lolling through those old hours.
I fancied slumber but, later,
couldn't sleep for all the coveting of it.

Originally, three muses: song, occasion, memory;
the voice singing, the moment and reason for utterance,
and the recalling of it after. How convenient
that the field opened up before me;
how thankful I am that room was made for me.
Consequence is not only what is borne

but also what is borne out—and so,
we carry on, we carry on so.

# Author's Bio

**Anna Leahy** is the author of the poetry books *Aperture* and *Constituents of Matter* as well as this and two other chapbooks. She also wrote the nonfiction book *Tumor* and co-wrote *Conversing with Cancer* and *What We Talk about When We Talk about Creative Writing*. Her poems and essays have appeared at *The Atlantic, Buzzfeed, Comstock Review, Crab Orchard Review, Fifth Wednesday Journal, The Southern Review, The Pinch, The Rumpus,* and elsewhere, and her essays won the top awards from *Ninth Letter* and *Dogwood* in 2016. She directs the MFA program in Creative Writing at Chapman University, where she edits the international poetry journal *TAB* and curates the Tabula Poetica reading series. See more at www.amleahy.com.

# The Fire Circle

by

# Karen L. George

# Table of Contents

| | |
|---|---|
| Acknowledgments | 30 |
| Meeting Place | 31 |
| Grace | 32 |
| The Dead Live at Hemlock Lodge, Natural Bridge, Kentucky | 33 |
| Erosion | 34 |
| Past Life Flash at Feast of the Flowering Moon, Chillicothe, Ohio | 35 |
| Three Tenors | 36 |
| Visitation in ICU | 37 |
| Inscription in *Frida Kahlo's Masterpieces*, Half-Priced Books | 38 |
| Trees on my Way to Work and Back | 39 |
| Waiting for the light to change | 40 |
| Hiking Roan Mountain Haibun | 41 |
| Alaskan Cruise Haibun | 42 |
| Displaced | 43 |
| Recreation at Red River Gorge | 44 |
| *Vibrato* | 45 |
| Emergence | 46 |

# Acknowledgments

*94 Creations* "Trees on My Way to Work and Back"

*Blue Lyra Review* "Alaskan Cruise Haibun"

*Border Crossing* "*Vibrato*," "The Dead Live at Hemlock Lodge, Natural Bridge, Kentucky"

*Inner Passage* (Red Bird Chapbooks, 2014): "Waiting for the light to change," "Grace," "Re-creation at Red River Gorge, Kentucky," and "Emergence"

*Naugatuck River Review* "Visitation"

*Permafrost* "Waiting for the light to change"

*Star 82 Review* "Inscription in *Frida Kahlo's Masterpieces,* Half-Priced Books"

*Swim Your Way Back* (Dos Madres Press, 2014): "Waiting for the light to change," "Trees On My Way to Work and Back," "Alaskan Cruise Haibun," "Grace," "Hiking Roan Mountain Haibun," "Displaced," "Recreation at Red River Gorge, Kentucky," "*Vibrato,*" and "Emergence"

*Sugar Mule* "Grace," "Feasting"

*Sugared Water* "Displaced"

*The Journal of Kentucky Studies* "Re-creation at Red River Gorge, Kentucky"

*The Seed of Me* (Finishing Line Press, 2015): "The Dead Live at Hemlock Lodge, Natural Bridge, Kentucky"

# Meeting Place

Hiking high on a ridge, a clearing in the storied forest. Flat river rocks on the ground in an arc— Moon come to Earth. You inch off the path. A deeper silence settles. When you touch a tall hemlock, a hum, a flame rises in your root chakra. A key turns, you step back a century.

You've been here before. Seated in a fire circle, shadows on painted faces. You mouth words in a foreign tongue. Your thick black hair braided, hips narrow, no breasts. Scent of sage and sassafras swoon you.

Beneath your feet: bone fragments, scattered seeds.

# Grace

A friend sent her essay about a great blue heron that flew across her car's hood, so close she could have touched it without the windshield in the way. She lived near a river where they nested in treetops. Her family mired in crises, the bird-in-flight yanked her back. I thanked her, said her story salvaged me—you near the end, not eating, barely sipping, each day more skeletal. She vowed to send a heron our way. Two dawns later, on our lake bank—spindly legs, neck an elongated s-curve, bill like twin blades. I slowed, lowered my window, memorized the scruffy plume feathers, the black striped from eye to crown, and when it turned, its pale face. To tell you every detail. How my breath ebbed when I met its onyx gaze, how I became bodiless but for eyes, nose and ears, the lake water sweet and feral, the snap as the wings unlatched.

# The Dead Live at Hemlock Lodge, Natural Bridge, Kentucky

The first time   I felt the dead   among the living   I was ten, on a family vacation.  The dining room air   dusk-heavy, as though we trudged through waist-high water.  The dark wood of tables, chairs, wall and ceiling beams    dimmed the midday light from the bank of windows. I neither saw nor heard the passed, only felt their current, a pool.  No fear or torment, more like the salve of walking in woods   among tunneling insects    and roots. I knew not to tell, as I knew not to question   the nuns in school. To keep beliefs   and doubts hidden. I studied my parents' and sisters' faces, and buried the secret   in my soul. Not the place they said sin tarnished, but where the seed of me    burrowed, thinned, and branched.

# Erosion

On a frayed clothesline next door Mrs. Griebe hangs wash. Her blue-gray hair reminds me of a broken-down Brillo pad. Ribs have snapped loose from the willow basket at her feet. Clothespins clump in her calico apron pocket. One sheet holds a rust-red stain shaped like a sliver of moon—Mr. Griebe died in bed last year.

I smell potatoes, onions, carrots simmer, soften as broth clots. Earlier, through the kitchen window, she minced, right shoulder rocking up, down—crisp flesh cleft.

## Past Life Flash at Feast of the Flowering Moon, Chillicothe, Ohio

I inhale sage smoke, feel grass blades tickle, the cool May ground rumble with the Native American dance—leap and lunge of feathered headdresses, shirts, capes, and aprons adorned with beads, fringe, and ribbons

my vision curls closed like the end chamber of a kaleidoscope rotates, spirals to a point of no light, a silent scene appears as on a movie screen, swatches of blurred motion focuses to a girl behind an Indian on a horse, flanks wet, buckskin pants, a calico dress, her open mouth, the scream slams into my chest, smothered by the man's knotted back, tang of dried mud and sweat, tips of his hair lash my cheeks, hooves pound the ground, the snort of nostrils, I taste dust and blood, hooves hair mud sweat knots buckskin calico blur

my vision unfurls into a kaleidoscope of leap and lunge—beads, fringe, ribbons, feathers—cool May ground rumbles, grass blades tickle, I inhale sage smoke.

## Three Tenors

Whenever you stayed in the hospital you craved Carreras, Domingo, Pavarotti, since the first time your lung collapsed. Air inside your body cavity swelled you to a sumo wrestler. *Nothing to do*, they said, *no real danger*. But air huddled everywhere. So hot, you couldn't breathe, they ordered a fan but wouldn't let me bring one. So I fanned you with cardboard yanked from a legal pad. Invited you to imagine sledding downhill unclothed. *Feel ice particles you speed through,* I say, *At the slope bottom you roll off, face first. Feel how the snow caresses your skin, the sweet cold glides from your scalp to your toes.* You listen, eyes closed, while I trail you with ice slivers. When I insert the tape, their voices infuse the room, and you want them *louder, louder, louder* until their lung power enters you, lulls you in liquid notes.

# Visitation in ICU

A lull in our conversation. The air charged. Your gaze rose to the room's upper corner. *Mother,* your voice a broken whisper. You listened, nodded. I floated in the bath of that space. *Emeline*—your late sister.

You sat so still, angled forward to catch each word, face lit from a source I felt the aura of.

When the presence ebbed, you cried, said your mother wore the blue dress you remembered, introduced you to uncles gone before your birth.

I still wonder what they said, what you absorbed in your crown, eyes, ears, open mouth—cupped palms like conch shells resting on the shore of your sheets.

# Inscription in *Frida Kahlo's Masterpieces,* Half-Priced Books

Inside: cramped letters inscribed on the title page, signed *Heath, January 9th*—the day my husband died fifteen years ago. Addressed to *Miyuki*, the words so familiar, in Lou's voice: *I am certain of nothing but the holiness of the heart's affection, and the truth of the imagination*—Keats from a letter to a friend. While *Bright Star* credits rolled, the actor recited "Ode to a Nightingale" in a whisper. Like John and Fanny, I imagine Heath and Miyuki lovers. He gave her the art book on their anniversary. But she never liked Frida's art; its rawness reminded Miyuki of botched love.

The pages virginal, turned by me only. I feel Heath's fervor buying the book, his joy as Miyuki rips speckled tissue, touches the cover, mouths the words inside—the only time she opens the book. On her cocktail table like an albatross—one more thing she never explores. But I want to linger on the moment she sees her lover's cursive, loops she follows across the page. I see her seated, eyes closed, palms pressed to Frida's face as Heath speaks the words he knows by heart.

## Trees on my Way to Work and Back

The redbud by our driveway in spring dangled purple balls that opened heart-shaped leaves. Across the street, twin magnolias, dark leathery leaves. Two doors up, sweet gums—five-lobed leaves pointed like stars, plus spiked fruitballs in fall. Cottonwoods at the stop sign floated white puffballs mid-summer. Thorny locusts arched over the big bend—contorted branches, sweet swags near Mother's Day, long seedpods later. Where crows gathered at dusk. At the five-way light, an Osage-orange whose knobby globes Dad swore repelled spiders. Catalpas as I turned right then left before the Chinese elm strung with strands of clear lights in the dregs of winter dawn. The avenue edged with Bradford pears that cascaded a sea of confetti, and when I emerged from their shade tunnel, a linden, its concrete prison raised by roots. Near the bridge a stand of aged sycamores flanked the river, mottled trunks, nests only visible in winter. At workday's end, I couldn't wait to see my first glimpse of the backyard Newport plum, crown above my roof, leaves the color of merlot. My route for 23 years.

When I moved in with you, my new commute began and ended with water maples, livid yellow leaves we loved to rake. Then our condo further south, the stately beech in the field I circled on the exit ramp, its twin across the road at a lot's edge where I spotted deer. The old burr oak razed to expand the school. I still superimpose its gnarled silhouette over the bricks every time I pass.

# Waiting for the light to change

in the curb lane, minutes from home, a van crashes into the side of my Honda Civic. Thinking *my ankle*, broken two years ago, I hobble out to a woman who claims a man waved her on, the way clear. Police arrive, reports are taken, cars towed. Home from Emergency, just a jam, I wander our rooms, open mail, try not to replay the impact, the sound of metal crushed, torn, quiet severed by pings of recoil. Tasks and consequences tick off–*call your agent, take off work, rent a car, visit body shop, owe deductible, premium will escalate, policy cancel.* In the new condo only a week, I weigh our decision to move. Pace, breathe. Through the sliding glass, dim in late dusk, a spotted fawn on the hill crest ten feet close. From the open window: crush of leaf pulp, huff of nostrils. *Turn,* I will its way. The head swivels, the white throat tenses, and I swim in the pool of its dark eyes, the pale pink caves of its ears.

# Hiking Roan Mountain Haibun

Thunderstorms are serious here, but the forecast claims no rain. The trail, in places only a foot wide, writhes between dense forest, neck-high grasses, boulders. Broken leg healed, I still clench the fear of falling, my body tight even as I try to stay loose. When we reach the crest, wind spikes, lightning veins. I ask you to lead the way down, promise to keep up, eyes rooted to your calves toned from Taekwondo. Gravid legs, ragged breaths, I think *Let the damn lightning strike me.* But we beat the downpour. At a town cafe, our waitress says earlier that year lightning killed four generations picnicking on that bald mountain.

This time you save me
but when cells accumulate
who can redeem you?

# Alaskan Cruise Haibun

They opened the grand dining room doors to unveil the midnight buffet, and passengers poured through the cloud of disinfectant like flies zooming. Nauseated, I leaned to inhale the scent of ginger tablets you chewed for motion sickness. We moved with the mass, past banquet tables glutted. Jockeyed for photos of Neptune and Venus chiseled from ice. Radish roses. Doves coddled from carrots, raw potatoes and turnips dyed and cut into cockatoos and bald eagles. Watermelon birds of paradise, honeydew hummingbirds, cantaloupe parrots, peacocks with fantails of fruit shish-kabobs. An octopus of icing beneath dark chocolate palm trees. Butter sculpted into whales, sea lions, pirates and mermaids. Liver pate molded into fat-bellied spiders. When my mind veered to the wet pulp of a spider flattened on hardwood, I fought the gag reflex, forced a smile to match everyone's wonder. But the cocoon of oohs and aahs could not protect me from the memory of all the food you failed to keep down—only one way chemo defiled you. We reached the end. Thin-sliced meats (already turning) cascaded like ocean waves.

With a champagne toast
we pushed through the dark waters,
the Inner Passage.

# Displaced

When I returned home from where I spoke the poem of our cruise before you died, moonlight unveiled a shadow on the living room floor. Thinking *large spider,* I stiffened, sucked in my breath, touched the grained leather of the hall console, tiptoed until I made out the wooden heart I'd wedged in a crook of driftwood a foot from the wide mantel's edge. I lifted the heart to my palm's plane. Stared at the nude branch, tried to fathom the heart's dislodge, the roll off. No fan on, no window open, no nearby vent. The heart was heavy and hot—smooth balsam striated in twin curves—its narrow bottom pointed to my wrist, the plump top nestled where fingers formed. I believed you'd held it seconds before I opened the door. That if I walked through the portal of the bedroom we shared, I'd find you.

## Recreation at Red River Gorge

I stand before the chasm, camera aimed, *battery exhausted* flashing. On my last vacation day, I'd found the path, but only a hand-wide swath of water sluiced down the rock faces that fit together like puzzle pieces: grays and tans, some moss furred, veined black, pocked or mottled, edges rounded by the flow. The scents of soil, vegetation, water scoured by stone lull me back to the time I stood before the same waterfall, then a five foot wide surge. You climbed and straddled slabs half-submerged to stand near where the cascade landed. And wanted me to follow, but short legs and fear of falling held me back. So I framed you with the tumbling plunge, the aura of mist, the boulders, loosed over time, kneeling at the base like worshippers.

## *Vibrato*

> "The greatest thing you'll ever learn is just to love and be loved in return."
> — From "Nature Boy," sung by Nat King Cole, heard in the movie *Untamed Heart*

I almost didn't attend the reading, didn't want to deal with freeway repair, traffic clogged to one lane for miles. Instead, wound my way through back roads, old neighborhoods, sloshed through time and memory past the persons I once was. To poets who read moving lines, pleas, rants, and a female friend who sang "Nature Boy" *a cappella* in clear, sweet notes that echoed Nat King Cole's deep-voiced version inside me.

I first heard the song in a film's final scene, where a woman played a record given by her lover who died of a defective heart. While the poet sang, I saw the actress lower the needle to the turntable, hug the album cover to her heart, eyes closed.

A week before you died, you pulled out music I never knew you owned, from before we met. As the vinyl spun, you listened your way back.

## Emergence

When I dust the porcelain angel nosing the rubber Rottweiler, I recall your story of the night you took your service revolver to bed. Your second marriage failed, your father dead, an ugly lawsuit pending. You knew where to aim, but your dog wouldn't look away. Would not budge from the door you couldn't haul open. Onto the bed you fell. Enveloped, in a great body of water. Became a body of water. Fourteen hours later you woke when your dog nuzzled your neck. You never forgot that rush, you said, of rising from a liquid abyss, as if the first creature to clamber onto shore.

When I think of you at that time of despair, I see you surge from the sea, as in the scene* where a mute woman unknots herself from a piano dragging her to the ocean floor, pierces the surface, is lifted into a boat. I think of your death that way, how you breached this life, frailties trickling off you like crystals.

* The movie *The Piano*, released in 1993, directed by Jane Campion, the mute woman played by Holly Hunter.

# Author's Bio

**Karen L. George** is author of five chapbooks, most recently an ekphrastic collaborative chapbook, *Frame and Mount the Sky* (Finishing Line Press, 2017), and two poetry collections from Dos Madres Press, *Swim Your Way Back* (2014) and *A Map and One Year* (2018). Her work has appeared in *Adirondack Review, Naugatuck River Review, Louisville Review, Sliver of Stone, Heron Tree*, and *Still: The Journal*. She received grants from Kentucky Foundation for Women and Kentucky Arts Council, and holds an MFA in Writing from Spalding University. She reviews poetry and interviews poets at Poetry Matters: http://readwritepoetry.blogspot.com/, and is co-founder and fiction editor of the online journal,
*Waypoints:* http://www.waypointsmag.com/.

# Letters to my Daughter

by

# Robert Perry Ivey

# Table of Contents

| | |
|---|---|
| Acknowledgment | 52 |
| Author's Note | 53 |
| Father's First Spring | 55 |
| When You Were Born | 56 |
| Ritual Analog | 57 |
| The River Shares Her Secrets | 58 |
| Hummingbird | 60 |
| Letter To Tally Bryant Ivey | 61 |
| Speaking Crow | 63 |
| The Origin of Christmas Trees | 66 |
| Jesus Was a Georgia Boy | 68 |
| A Plausible Explanation to my Daughter for What Happens After We Die | 69 |
| First Poem | 70 |
| Tattoos: Summoning the Self | 72 |
| Lullaby | 74 |

# Acknowledgment

*Blue Lyra Review* "Letter to Tally Bryant Ivey"

# Author's Note

For Exie, my firstborn, my little light, my morning glory, my evening star,

Some of these are epistolary poems and lullabies that I have read and sung a million times while rocking you to sleep. Those you will know. Some of these are lessons, some observations, and some are confessions that you will read later when you begin to think that the world is full of nothing but pain and death and offal scum and political stomach vile, which have all turned the world into unreality that is hardly bearable to thinking, decent humans. Those confessions you will not know. Those are about your sister, Tally, our first, but not our firstborn.

In the event that I am no longer here when you are old enough to read this, know that you are loved from wherever I am; even if it is in the hereafter or great nothing, you are loved like hummingbirds love flowers, crows love corn, grandmamas love their grandbabies, and like the way daddies should love their daughters. If you ever find yourself looking hard into a mirror or lake, or staring out to sea or down a river, or in pain that cuts to the soul, read this. It will not give you any answers or tell you how to live, but it will tell you that I love you.

## Father's First Spring

*after the Avett Brother's "Father's First Spring"*

Dear Exie Marie Ivey,

Daddy couldn't get drunk off the wine of living anymore,
built a tolerance to it and always knew
there was a crow riding on his shoulder. These days, that damn
black bird casts a long and greedy-dark shadow. So, when I fly
to the family-lover-friend light,
I want to have left you words, baby doll, that say
I have not left you.    I held you once
in one hand, fingertips to elbow nook, and you ruined
my heart for the rest of my life. I held you once
and whenever I could after. You made me feel the world
in silk and velvet, and wild and terrible awe,
the way I got high
spinning circles as a kid, jumping out of swings
into mountains of leaves and wrapping paper, ribbon, cake,
and story-time. Baby girl,
when the whole world swirled reasons to hate,
when the news, the politicians, cops and robbers
sneered, snarled, and scarfed up every nickel and dime innocent,
you made me love and see music in color again.
Not even if I drowned the sun in the sea barehanded, not even
 if I squeezed the moon to silver dust, chalk powder and glitter
shine, not even if I wove all flowers, vines, stars, streams,
and colored twine into my eyes, would you know
how much I love you. But you will, when you bloom
a life of your own, you will know
just how much you ruined my heart
for the rest of all time.

# When You Were Born,
                        6/20/12-

It was the year of the dragon, the summer solstice,
the longest day, the shortest night.  It was the dawn
when spring's thighs loosened to summer's flower
and blaze, when earth turns its shaggy head to the sundial's tune,
when you were born, baby girl,
the sun poured its pastel liquor through the window,
bathing you and Julie who cradled and sang:
*Red and yellow and pink and green,*
*purple and orange and blue,*
Julie sang a rainbow,
Julie sang a rainbow to you just as she had
when you were a bump, a lump, a spot,
when you were a speck of a speck, and you
instantly calmed by *Somewhere Over,*
when you were born, that switch they tell you about,
the one you can never understand, flips on love
like velvet on a dry tongue, strong like
love for the first time, but now, every day,
something closer than the words we have for all that is good,
something pure, for once:
your eyes, blue like glacial ice,
eyes like the full moon behind cobblestone clouds,
when you were born.

# Ritual Analog

When you get old enough,
I want you to light an antique oil lamp,
take one of my old records from the cedar chest,
blow the dust off, and gently,
the way you hold a candle-lit cake, the way you hold
your first driver's license,
or a tray of communion wine shot glasses in a Baptist church,
with both hands and a slow walk,
place a record, whose album art speaks to you, on the altar.

With both fingers, let the needle kiss the vinyl and sing.
Learn to love analog. Be amazed
at the way a simple needle, on simple grooves, dips, and bumps,
miniature trenches, can play every vocal, every strummed string,
percussion pop, splash, and tink,
every bass thump and trumpet blare, an orchestras' worth
of instruments
all at once.

I want you to love analog. So
when you are old enough,
light that oil lamp I bought from a yard sale
from Trisha Yearwood's grandparents, pour a glass of red wine,

play that record, put that needle to the groove and sing.
Make some analog of your own:
perhaps, paint or play guitar, or like Daddy,
put pen to paper and bleed, bleed ink
blossoms, learn the obvious, learn the obscure
and write it beautiful
like the man who polished a cross section of a 100 year old oak,
set it on a record player and, for the first time ever,
let us hear a century of drought,
flood, forest fire, and sunshine in a tree's low whale song.

# The River Shares Her Secrets

Every time I wrap my hands around the paddle's wooden wrist,
or yoke, or bow and soundlessly slip into the water,
or lay my hands flat
and slide them over the river's skin,
she tells me a secret.

March means going mad with wanting to fish
and water churns muddy from thaw, not yet
she licks into my ear.

In April, she tells me that the poplars' orange and yellow blooms
float down the river like vespers,
like Willy Wonka candy cups, freshly cut, funeral flower gardens
put out to sea by the red-bellied stranger.
Dogwood blooms mean catfish and bream are running;
she smells slutty, like fish and perfume.

In May, she says mountain laurels draw butterflies to banks
colors in flight reflect below Cherokee roses
spreading their white thighs
on the river's sandy lips. Bass run hot and cold, feed hard
and then fend beds of orange-marble eggs.

June, July, and August are all the same:
the world, even the shade, feels like an open oven door,
and the river rubs its aloe fingers on my skin

while black turtle shells dot logs
like rows of German helmets peaking over trenches.
Dog days mean violence, mean the occasional floating body
belly up like a sick one eyed moon. This killer's secret,
she keeps all to herself.

Every September, sweet gums shower their dandelion snow,
the river looks like peach fuzz on a dirty virgin's hips, faerie fluff
blankets the top water. The mud loses its heavy silt smell;
the suckhole hides the body.

October turns sweet again, bass feed up,
fatten for winter, she swirls leaves in a fire of orrery whirlpools
beside blankets of tree confetti pressing the water flat
with reds and yellows that once stroked the wind.

By November, leaves put on their makeup
and the river water stands so still and flat, if you look into her,
she stares and stares right back and tells her secrets.

I have been tempted to throw it all down
into a fire pit of fuck it, I have tightrope walked the lip
of Flatbridge with nothing left to lose, her break up rocks below,
and stared into that river. She didn't give me any answers,
but stared back and told me:

*The snake does not hate the hawk, some young girls*
*have kissed naked on the sandbar,*
*like a child, the moon splashed their breast*
*with mercury colored water,*
*drink from me, fish from my thighs while you can,*
*while damsel flies still light on cane poles*
*because come January and February,*
*when waterfalls ice my beard and trees on one side,*
*I make love to Mr. Death and smile*
*just like a virgin.*

## Hummingbird

Why do hummingbirds like flowers so much
and fly so fast, baby girl? Is that what you asked? Well,
scientists say they evolved on a sugar diet,
making them the A.D.H.D. children of the bird world;
the Taino believe the Sun Father turned flies into hummingbirds
to spread life over the earth. And,
all this is true.

                But, I'll tell you baby girl, this truth;
                Hummingbird, he's a romantic.

He loves color,                                        tastes
color, chases blossom fall and violet shivers, races blooms up
and down the world,             beats Spring,     calls dibs
on the best spots for romancin' other birds
where flowers first flush and pop       open,
                       plunges his beak face first into
whatever pretty little flower petal         comes
his way,         and buzz-whir-machinegun-chirp-and-twit
        he's pitched over sipping orange,     face first
into yellow,              slurping up pink and blue,
and he sees rainbow shades we could never see,    that glow
in soul-colored-hue.
                 Because he loves flower-color so much,
                            he grew prism feathers to
wash, to paint, to diffract
     light into his  green wings and blossomed throat shining
petal-plant-red          like the slit throat of first love.
Daddy loves Exie girl like Hummingbird loves color,
              and if Daddy lost you,
                he would be colorblind, baby girl,
                                a
hummingbird,
          with only one wing
                           left.

## Letter to Tally Bryant Ivey

Before you were born, I loved you;
before you were born, I killed you
like a mama dog bites in half puppy heads of imperfect pups.
I bought you "Lovey the Lamb" blankets,
"Daddy makes me smile" bibs,
and seersucker Easter dresses with azalea colors.
Both sides of the family painted your room spring green
with angel cream trim, and I made a white hanging basket
that held an African violet beside the window.

I tell myself that it was for medical reasons,
the Trisomy, the C.F., that I would not risk my wife's life
for an imperfect baby, and all that is a truth.

But I confess to you now
that I could have never fully afforded you,
loved you the way a born sick baby needs.
Some animal part of me
bared its teeth,
loved, detested, despised, and pitied you
back to the nothing.

I took you somewhere good, to someone
who would end you humanely, decently, tenderly.

And I confess this as well;
they asked us if we wanted to have a service
for your too little body.

We said no,
let the doctors give you the mercy pyre
with all the rest of the throw-aways,
and I am so sorry for that baby girl,
so sorry that you deserved what we couldn't face.

I planned to burn your sonogram pictures,
and spread the ashes in a clean river, to speak your name,
Tally Bryant Ivey, for the last time, but I couldn't even walk onto
that bridge.

My first, but not my firstborn,
this is the last time
that I will ever say your name,
but not the last time
that I will go on punishing myself
until I see you again in the after.

## Speaking Crow

I don't dream
anymore.  I don't pray
anymore, haven't in a few years,
not since the crow first landed on my shoulder
and whispered into my left ear.
He was so black
he shimmered black, sparkled and shined
black.  And in that cackling gurgle croak
and prehistoric caw
told me my dark secret, told me
the world's darkest secret,
and I began to speak crow.
I remember every moment
I ever saw a crow, each time
I ever began to speak a little crow,
a few words at first
like the caw I learned when some punk kid
gut shot my first dog, the call I imitated
after my first broken heart.
I once worked in a pet store.  A great
red parrot outlived its owner and pulled
and plucked out every feather it could reach
leaving bald and grey ash skin pimpled
and wrinkled except on its head
and between the shoulder blades.
It pined itself to death the same way Johnny Cash went
within six months of June Carter.
I learned to speak crow.

I started to see crows everywhere,
every day, a shadow through the trees
corner-eye and chalkboard caw, a crow on an old cedar post,
a murder of crows sitting slant-back and curved like cursive
and voodoo music notes slumped on power lines,
lining my page, an ink blot blossoming into flight.
I carried corn in my pocket.
I learned to speak crow.

Soon, I saw them when others did not:
during our first ultrasound, on the monitor
when the nurse took too long looking at our daughter's neck,
at Tally's neck, and the nurse's eyes teared, and the nurse
ran out, the doctor came in, I saw the crow
in the screen, in the chromosome and cyst, black
and greedy. I learned to speak crow.

I saw a crow on the windowsill when we aborted her,
for medical reasons, but still,
aborted. I heard a crow cawing
when we decided not to have a funeral,
when we tried to let it slip away
like painkillers into black moonshine.
I wanted my wife to play the wishing game again,
and the crow was there, calling from a little velvet lined box,
from black and white squares,
and I saw the crow when I snuck out that Christmas
and burned the ultrasound pictures by the old grist mill,
buried them under a rock, spread
the rest of the ashes into the black ribbon
of the Towaliga River.
I learned to speak crow.

That week I killed 13 crows a day.
I could talk them right into the yard
shoot them out of the suicide tree,
and it didn't matter to me if they carried a grudge, if they might
refuse to carry my soul across the river when I die.
The crow still came anyway, landed on my shoulder, whispered
into my left ear secrets darker than my first daughter's death.
I will speak a little crow for you now, just one
black secret it told me, the sickest joke of all,
and if you heard it in true crow,
you would shudder-jerk with a stiff neck crack
and rub your face in grief.

The crow spoke this:
*We are all already dead.*
*This Is Heaven. This Is*
*our Second Chance, and my God,*
*we pissed on it too. We do not*
*deserve our souls.*

## The Origin of Christmas Trees

Some people forgot
Christmas has nothing to do with Christ,
who wasn't even born in winter,
Christians, presents, or even Santa.  Some
think they know, but they have forgotten down in their bones
where it all started.
Before there was ever Christmas, hundreds of years ago,
those northern Europeans went about business as usual,
summer, fall, winter, and spring,
fish and gather, harvest and hunt, survive and shiver, plant
and breed again year after year until
one winter
snow fell.  As usual,
folks stayed warm, bundled babies, put fire warmed rocks
under sheets and furs before slipping into sleep,
and waited the cold out.
But, snow still fell, the grey covered the sky, the cold
curled up like a dog at their bone marrow's feet
the year spring did not return.

First the sickly froze, then the old:
old folks, old dogs.  Then
the young: babies, kids, puppies, year after year
people prayed
to anything green, for spring green again,
and people quit having babies to bundle.
They made up dozens of new words for snow
and new gods of ice, fire, and trees
and prayed for light and flowers and birdsong.

After years,
they looked to the only thing still evergreen.
They brought fir limbs in by the armloads
and lined cabin-nests with holly boughs, like bowery birds
they tucked pine into every corner, made holly infinity symbols
and cedar circle garlands, stuffed spruce in breezy wall holes.
Hundreds of bee wax candles hung like
tanned bones from the rafters and eventually
folks brought whole dang trees in.
Then, things got bad.
Quarters and halves and wholes of villages passed on.
The ones left prayed to pines. They adorned firs with offerings:
gifts wrapped in spring colors; blue and red berries, some
even poisonous; ribbon and twine; hundreds
of candles in hopes that the big light, life, spring
would bloom again.  After so many years of praying to green, of bringing in
trees, of covering them with candles,
the clouds broke, birds returned, and there was color
again.  By then, those folks that were left
just kept on toting in trees, scared to death
that the long winter would come again
and that the whole world could be that cold in its bones.

Folks today still bring trees in baby girl; even if
they have forgotten why, their bones still remember
the decade long winter.  And baby girl,
even when people don't remember why, even if it is just a tree
and muscle memory to them now, people will pray to any damn thing
when their backs are to the wall.

## Jesus Was a Georgia Boy

Let me tell you
"The Legend of the Dogwood," baby girl:

They once rivaled the height of any poplar, pine, or spruce.
In the old days, one dogwood was so thick
it took three grown men to link their arms around its trunk.

And way back when,
some bad, bad men nailed Lord Christ Almighty Jesus to a
dogwood cross, baby girl.

And God, in His great wisdom, didn't curse the men. Oh, noooo.
No, He had already done that in the garden,
but He did curse the dogwood trees,
and all the dogwoods that ever would be.

That's why the four white petals grow red at the tips,
fold and tear a hole
in the petal's palm just before they fall.

Now, their flowers bleed, their limbs are
gnarled and stunted so small
that they can never make a cross again big enough for His son.

Now, I know your teacher says,
"There are no dogwoods in Israel."
Well, never you mind that talk.
Everybody knows Jesus was a Georgia boy anyhow.

# A Plausible Explanation to my Daughter for What Happens After We Die

Our blood is 92% water baby girl, our bodies 75;
though we are eyelash, blood, bone, little piggy toes,
those parts are made of water just like

every sweet potato plant, stink bug, tomato stick,
blue bird on a wire, and cat stalking through wheat grass
is made of water, lives and dies by it.

And baby girl, lady moon,
who pours the color of your eyes onto the nighttime pastures,
who pushes and pulls tides with her full and empty tummy,
one day,

the moon will push and pull the water inside you.
Baby girl, scientists in your little books
say water has memory, say two molecules of water that have met,

that dove inside the same drop, landed on a tongue as a snowflake,
that dried up and drifted off on the wind
are more likely to meet
and bond again in the same rainbow mist, rain-ping on a tin roof,
or roll off the same rubber ducky's back.

Our blood is 92% water, baby girl, and water has memory.
When we die, baby girl, Mommy
and Daddy's water will find you again, and we will run rivers,
leap from waterfalls, live in clouds, and fill every fish with air.

# First Poem

Baby Girl,
Let me tell you about the time
the first words were spoken, the first poem was ever written.
Once upon a long long time ago,
some tribesman were slouched squirrel-backed
over a set of deer tracks like two by two teardrops in the mud,
One tribesman kept kneeling, and kneeling, studying
those tracks, his tracks, the tribe's footprints, symbols
of passings and goings old as earth's ebb, and he saw
the first story ever written.

His brothers sniff the wind and see
nothing. But, when he sees prints,
like lopsided clovers as big as his palm, join in
with the mud-story, the hairs on his neck,
back, forearms stand on end, and he tries, baby girl, tries
to warn them of the tooth and claw cat, but
there is no word for flight. Instead,
he makes a squeal that signifies nothing
but weakness, and one of his brothers gets gobbled up, slurp,
baby girl, and the rest jumped six feet up,
knees to chests, roll-scrambling down the hill in a ball of fur,
hairy arms, and broken sticks.

But the one tribesman, the one who sees the story,
followed the tooth-cat back to his hole,
and sleep-gutted that beast wide open with a flint knife,
pulled out his gobbled up brother, and they skinnt that kitty.

And when the two got back to the fire circle, those tribesman
liked'ta stone that story-reader half-to-death, thinking
he brought back their brother from the dead,
thinking he was half crazy,
half beast, him wearing that dread-cat's stripes like a headdress
and cape. And when he speaks, they cover their ears;
he makes prints in the sand.
They scream and kick dirt. And when he painted the story

on the cave wall, they cover their eyes.
And when he put that fanged skull
and cape on his head, and chased his brothers around the fire,
teeth gnashing and air scratching, making stabbing
and stomach cutting gestures, they only saw a parted maw
and bloody teeth.
They liked'ta beat him moon-eyed
trying to get away like monkeys jumping on the bed.
But, baby girl...
Years later, his son does what the father could not;
he teaches them
words and the great mud story, he becomes their shaman,
their historian, their holy-roller-dirt-road preacher, and he
becomes the first poet.
And the whole while, baby girl, the whole while
the women were sitting in a circle,
writing sonnets and talking up a storm.

## Tattoos: Summoning the Self

There is something true in us
which wants to peel back the skin
and say, *Hello.*
      Some of us
slink into to a tattoo parlor
and brave the blade to be a stranger's canvas:
the tough guys' tribals, proud parents with their children's names
on the inside of their lips or chest cursive trash, proud husbands
with their sugarpies' names (the soon-to-be divorcees), the easy girls
with tramp stamp targets right above their butts
(Dear Lord, don't get this tattoo, baby girl),
the fun girls
with pot-foggy butterflies
and swallows on their ankles next to gold toe rings
(and if that's the worst thing you'll ever be, baby girl,
you ain't doing so bad),
the goofy kid in grade school, who never ungoofed,
getting Looney Tunes on his lunch break,
the women my dad said "never date" getting any predatory reptile
or insect: black widow, black adder, praying mantis,
scorpion skeleton, skull and crossbones watch out mama.
And frat boys...
      Jesus God, the frat boys and their Greek letters.

But there are some of us who know
from having known
and felt the ancient awe of the artist and the symbol.
And we walk in, some of us with a why
and some us with a why the hell not,
needing a particular arrangement of blood, blade, and ink,
and we go to a stranger,
whose art has been practiced for a hundred thousand years,
and the artist summons something true of our self
from gritted teeth and blood magic, from the animal place of
symbol-thought.

For the buffoons, he conjures cartoons; the sluts,
tramp stamps; the gear heads, muscle cars;
the soldiers, bombshells and bullet holes; gangstas,
stupid thug shit; the youthfully dumb, regret;
and me, baby girl,
at the turn of the millennia, I draw a Chinese bone dragon.
I have a man named Little Rat summon it to my shoulder's surface,
and 13 years later, you are born
in the year of the dragon, summoned
from my very blood.

# Lullaby

I've read you books, I've sang you songs
the sky sends dewy weep
You're tucked under twenty blankets
Exie girl, it's time to sleep

The moon has been lain down to bed
the stars begin their shine
Spiders thread silk fishing lines
moonflowers bloom just one time
The sun will rise to greet you
trees will breath delight
your mother and I whisper
Goodnight, baby girl, goodnight

Luna dog curls at your feet
kit-cat is at your side
"Lovey Lamb" is in the crib
Goose took a trolley ride

Three, six, nine shouts the monkey
cow jumped o'er the moon
the three bears found three chairs
and licked the silver spoons
the oil lamp smiles a glow
and the wick is black and white
Bo'peep watches all his sheep
night, night, Exie girl, night night

The moss bed is velvet green
oaks bend to kiss your hair
In the petting zoo it's sleepy time
bulbs blink at the county fair

The blue birds have ceased their flight
their heads tucked under-wing
eyes and beaks are closed up tight
so dream your rainbow

your lady bug casts ceiling stars
while the fireflies flash their lights
Your mother and I love you so
Goodnight, baby girl, night,
night

# Author's Bio

**Robert Perry Ivey** was born in Forsyth, GA, grew up in Macon and is a Lecturer at Gordon State College. He was the Visiting McEver Chair of Poetry at the Georgia Institute of Technology. Ivey has earned a M.A.in English Literature from Georgia State University and a M.F.A from Sarah Lawrence College in Creative Writing. He is the author of the chapbook *Southbound*, recipient of Academy of American Poetry's John B. Santoianni Award, and his work has appeared in *Java Monkey Speaks: A Poetry Anthology, Louisiana Review, Live Oak Review, Terminus Magazine, Blue Lyra Review, TYCA Southeast*, and *Negative Capability Press's Anthology of Georgia Poets: Stone, River Sky*. He is married to actress/model/photographer Julie Jones Ivey.

# Critical Praise

**Anna Leahy** has written a seductive suite of persona poems in the voice of nineteenth-century model, painter and poet, Elizabeth Siddall. The narrator meditates on various aspects of her life, including posing, sketching, motherhood, her red hair and even the laudenum which eventually takes her life. Historically accurate, the poems give us a fresh, imaginative look at Siddal's inner life. One is reminded of Adrienne Rich's comments about re-vision, entering an old text from a new critical direction, being an act of survival. "Dream me up; imagine me new" Leahy writes in one poem, and I am grateful for these bright and skillfully wrought imaginings of a woman whose life was shaped by the tension of being both subject and object, artist and muse.—Sheryl St Germain

This latest collection by **Anna Leahy** takes the ekphrastic poem out of the stuffy confines of museums and studios and turns it into a means for discovery and revelation. These poems breathe life into their subjects with a delicate touch and a thrumming heart. Intelligent, finely wrought, concise and precise, the poems of Sharp Miracles truly are eye-openers in the best sense—I feel my relationship with art charged and changed upon reading this chapbook.—Allison Joseph

In **Karen L. George**'s *The Fire Circle,* worlds collide in transformative ways. The very real aspects of daily life—including the loss of a loved one—mingle with the beauty of nature and the ephemera of the spirit world. Mountain trails, bedrooms, and even buffets become portals to an inner realm where shape-shifting memories and meanings are found through the observations of a determinedly open heart. These prose poem meditations crackle with the heat of emotion and the light of intuition. —Rochelle Hurt

In **Karen L. George**'s Prepare to be transported. *The Fire Circle* is a collection grounded in place, whether in muddy nature or a sterile ICU or a discount bookstore. Karen George takes you with her to all of these environs and more, in prose poems that are rooted in natural rhythms and lush description. What the poet offers is a frank look around, and it is a look that lovingly takes in everything, then hands it to you in its purest form on the page. These are poems that reward repeated attention. —Karen Craigo

**Robert Perry Ivey** explores the landscapes, the narratives, and the grotesques of the South, and, in something as genuine and bare as a loving lullaby from a father to a daughter, this book digs up the overlooked or forgotten truths behind seemingly ordinary, unquestioned things like Christmas trees, analog records, and the memory contained in water. Most importantly, Ivey's poetry evokes the marvelous complexities of a place often dismissed as simple by those who have never been there or spent much time there. –Stephen Roger Powers


In **Robert Perry Ivey**'s latest collection, *Letters to my Daughter*, he eloquently writes a book of love poems to a first-born daughter. It is also a book of elegy, of fierce promises, and of fierce hope. An original and wonderful book! —Thomas Lux

www.ingramcontent.com/pod-product-compliance
Lightning Source LLC
Chambersburg PA
CBHW032209040426
42449CB00005B/510